MW01343559

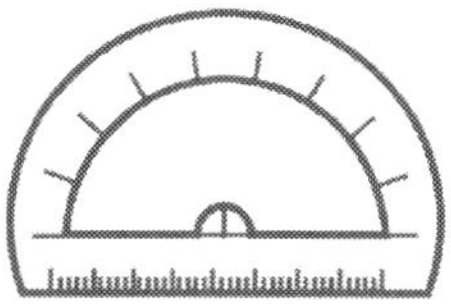

MATH NOTE BOOK

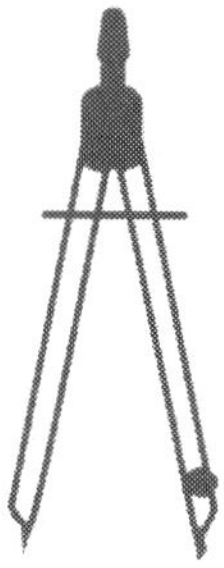

Name :

Subject :

Grade :

Made in the USA
Middletown, DE
30 August 2024

60013466R00068